Remember the Good Times

The information address

J2B Publishing LLC
4251 Columbia Park Road
Pomfret, MD 20657
www.J2BLLC.com
GladToDoIt@gmail.con

This book is set in Garamond
Cover Photograph by Benjamin Yates Brewster, Jr.

IBSN: 978-1-948747-77-6

Remember the Good Times

Richard I. Gold

J2B PUBLISHING

Also by Richard I. Gold

God's Agenda: Religious Poems Vol. I
Mary's Lamb and other Christmas Poems
God's Love - Easter Poems
Sayings for the Believers
The Wall and Other Poems
My Ghost and Other Poems
Work is a 4-Letter Word
Free Advice
Life is a Trip
The Tree of Salvation
Christmas Trees and Mistletoe
Cost of the Cross
My Ghost

Dedication

My thanks for the support from my wife Penelope Gold, and to those who have reviewed these poems and made valuable suggestions.

Table of Contents

INTRODUCTION

The future is a land where we must go. When we get there for others our existence will be what others will think of us when our name is mentioned. So we should be careful when we interact with others and try to make a good impression.

HOW WOULD YOU BE REMEMBERED?

How would you be remembered?
What would you have others say?
When you are no longer here
On your funeral day

What people remember of you
What do you wish them to know
This will be your legacy
As into the future they go

There are many things
That I would have of them
"In life he loved us
In death we love him"

WE OFTEN ARGUE WHAT WE BELIEVE

We often argue what we believe
About right and wrong
We bring much to the table of life
Before we are gone

Some life is of infinite worth
Some you can buy for a song
On leaving this life
They go like a ringing gong

Is it wrong to steal?
To take what is not yours?
Are things there for the taking?
No questions, no guilt, no tears

Some shoot up on drugs
Desire to flake out
Others would not touch the stuff
Have a life strong and stout

Does it matter what a teenager believes
Yet an adult too
It does not change the facts
But changes what they do

WALK THE LINE

Walk the line
But never cross
The line is the divide
Between profit and loss

Lines we draw
In the sands of time
We choose to cross or not
The future there is mine

For there are lines in life
When once we cross
There is no return
We have a new boss

Let us be aware
When we cross the line
The other side to behold
For what is on the other side
May swallow us whole

WE WALK A LINE

We walk a line
Between life and death
The living goes from here to there
Sometimes narrow, sometimes great width

Stay on the line
Do not let it end
For when we reach the conclusion
We cannot begin again

The line sets limits
Limits on what we may do
We must walk the line
We must be ever true

WE WALK THE WALK OF LIFE

We walk the walk of life
We cannot know the end
The question we must ask
"How do we begin?"

To know the beginning
The direction we must go
Is for us in life
All we need to know

Yet the end is important
Must ever be our goal
For it makes us who we are
Determines the fate of our soul

CHANGE IS IN THE WIND

Change is in the wind
Change is in the works
Change is coming
No matter whom it irks

Change is the product of time
It is forever with us
If we cannot change when we must
It will cause our life to "bust"

So go with the flow
Bend with change
For when the winds blow
It has you in its range

SPECIAL DAYS OF OUR LIVES

Special days of our lives
Are ones that make us so
They build the memories we have
Constitute what we know

But everyday things
Build up our total self
The breathing, eating, drinking
Are what constitutes our being

The important things we do
Are not what they generally seem
They are where we live
Are what our life doth mean

LISTEN, MY LITTLE ONE

Listen, my little one
There's something you should know
Saying something's true
Does not make it so

People say many things
About both great and small
Sometimes it's true
Sometimes not true at all

So when something you hear
It sounds so good
Weigh the truth of it
Believe what you should

Find a foundation
Upon which to build your life
Know it to be stable
You must have no strife

So always remember
As in everything you do
To many things help
But to yourself be ever true

A SHORT TIME WE LIVE

A short time we live
Our mark to be made
To build or to destroy
The price to be paid

The important things
That we put stock in
Will turn to dust
When we reach our end

But to those we leave
Who come after us
We leave a legacy
Greater than things that rust

DISCIPLINE YOURSELF

Discipline yourself
Do what you don't want to do
The harder it is
The better for you

Discipline your body
To straighten your soul
By doing this thing
Keeps you young not old

Discipline your mind
To know what to do
If you do not
It could be bad for you

Discipline your behavior
No lines cross
Someday, if you try
You will become the boss

THERE'S A LINE OF HUMANITY

There's a line of humanity
That runs through all history
A line that leads to a more humane world
Ideas that helps us human be

These lines were set by others
Our society and our kin
There is a set of rules
That tells us how to begin

The lines are to us a way
To live and to endure
That when we live life
We can make our way pure

YOU WALK A FINE LINE

You walk a fine line
Between wrong and right
No one wants to be wrong
No one wants to lose the fight

If we are not constrained by the line
To keep the way of right
We will find that we lose our way
As we face another's might

Unless we win
Unless we prevail
The memory of us will grow dim
Our life will grow frail

WINNING AND LOSING

There is winning and losing
And how we play the game
There are those who say
In the end it's all the same

This may be true
For those who do not play
But for those involved
WIN - there's no other way

But in the long run
When many years have passed
The final judgment is made
There are other questions asked

For who are we
And what we do
Will cause our true selves
To finally shine through

ONCE A ROAD IS TRAVELED

Once a road is traveled
It is new no more
Once life's bridge is passed
It belongs to days of yore

What is always the new
Stretches the mind
New discoveries, new thoughts
We want of every kind

But we want what is not too new
For new beyond belief
Will cast the mind into a hole
Deep beyond relief

THE LONGEST DAY OF OUR LIFE

The longest day of our life
Is the day I would not see
It has both good and bad
It will impact what is new for me

It has hope and goodness
For those on whom it doth smile
Keeps us from the fray
By time and a mile

The longest day will come
Carry us to there
Both an end and a beginning
Best to take care

TODAY IS THE DAY

Today is the day
To have and to hold
The future is a murky mist
The past so old

Today is all we have
To make us what we will be
For life changes and grows
Like the limb of a tree

We grow into the future
To be all that we can be
Never reaching full potential
Never quite the height we see

Do what you can today
Hope for the best
When this day is done
You will find your rest

THERE ARE THINGS

There are things
That makes those "them"
Things that divide
For some it is her or him

But one might ask

Who are those that are "them"
This is a difficult task
Because if you have to ask
You are one of "them"

THERE ARE THINGS WE CAN REMEMBER

There are things we can remember
Things that are remembered of us
Sometimes it is good
Sometimes it raises a fuss

As life goes from day to day
Events go by
We can but try to do our best
We can but try

We should attempt
To do good once we've begun
This is how we will be remembered
When life's race we've run

TODAY IS WHERE WE ARE

Today is where we are
Take from us other things we know
If it were not so
We would on other paths go

Yesterday is where we were
Shadows of things in a blur
Events that are long gone
Things that were

Tomorrow is yet to be
Its form we cannot see
We should give thought to it
Because that is where we will be

WHAT HAVE YOU DONE TODAY?

What have you done today?
Of what you would you tell?
If asked in the light of day
Would shout, would yell

Often there is not much
That each of us do
That builds up and fortifies
That is kind and loving and true

How would you be remembered?
When you are no longer here
Would it be with love and kindness?
Or with loathing and fear?

What you do everyday
Is bounded by what you can
By what you are remembered
Is the race that your life ran

THE WISHING TREE

When I was a child
I wanted a tree
Whose fruit would come
To be a wish for me

I'd wish for many things
For gold and candy and cars
But finding a wishing tree
Was not in my stars

Now I am a man
I have come to be me
But still I'd like to have
A good old wishing tree

REMEMBER

In a million years
A million years and a day
When all the possessions we have
Are destroyed by fire, mold and decay

When our lives are gone
Our names forgotten too
What will remain
Is the good and evil we do

So go forth and do good
To all, both great and small
That when we are judged by our Maker
We will be loved by all

I SIT UPON THE BRINK OF LIFE

I sit upon the brink of life
I dare not be too bold
But ere I take the plunge
The future I will hold

The future is a murky place
With many dangers wrought
It is a place where we must go
Where souls are sold and bought

With each danger comes opportunity
With each test a hope
We must be prepared
Always be able to cope

Prepare for the future
To be all you can be
That by God's guiding light
The golden hope you'll see

THERE IS A WAY I MUST GO

There is a way I must go
The end I cannot know
Be it good or be it woe
The future is where I must go

In this way I must go
Many paths I could take
Choosing the right path
Will the future make

If I choose a path of ill
I will not a good end make
For by my actions
Others will my substance take

If I choose the path of light
The path that leads to good
My life will be a way of peace
Doing the best I could

A BILLION DOLLARS

If I had a billion dollars
A billion dollars and a dime
It could buy me many things
But it could not buy me time

Money can buy clothes
The house that I own
But it cannot buy me love
Or make my house a home

Love is in the giving
Of myself and my wealth
It is in the helping
That will be my eternal health

MAKE NO PROMISES YOU CANNOT KEEP

Make no promises you cannot keep
Make no commitments that you wish you had not
Make no pledges that through your being seep
Nor vows that will cause your soul to rot

Live life in the good day
That you may go and not stop
For with each wrong turn
Your future may hit a spot

But through your life hold steady
To the principles you know are true
Let your bonded word be known
That what you say, you will do

IF I HAD

If I had
If I were
If this had happened to me
I would use
I would be
I would experience harmony

But I have
But I am
But this has happened to me
Therefore I use
Therefore I am
Therefore it all depends upon me

EPITAPH

Cemeteries are dismal places
Filled with the dead
Although it'll someday be my home
It does not fill me with dread

On each grave there is a stone
That tells of the dead
Some have a comment
For the living to be read

On my stone I wish to have
A saying I hope is true
That will have applied to my life
And my memory too

"When I am dead and gone
I hope that men will say
'Here lived a person
Great in his day'"

But how I am remembered
By the living one and all
Is what I did for them
When it is eternity's call

IF I OWNED ALL THINGS

If I owned all things
It would not give me might
If I knew all things
It would not make me right

It is not what can ever be
For men upon this earth
For we must ever struggle
So it is from birth

But owning is not having
Having is not the goal
For if we are not good hearted
The future will take its toll

THOUGHTS

We have thoughts and words
We have ideas too
But the importance of ideas
Is in what we do

The thoughts we have
The words also
Are far outweighed by
The deeds we do

Deeds are the judgement of life
They go with us along the way
They sit on our soul
For the totality of eternal pay

So let us consider what we do
Consider what others will say
For we live our life
We will be on that day

THE END OF TIME TO SEE

The end of time
Is what I will never see
It may, it will come
When it does I wish not to be

The end of all we know
Will pass before our eyes
We may wish to keep it all
But it will us despise

We are all mortal
Made of flesh and blood
Continue forever we wish
Is what we'd be if we could

We may have an everlasting plan
To continue beyond this day
It is by faith and love
We will continue if we may

THE END OF TIME WILL COME

The end of time
Will come when it will
We cannot know when
It may be good or ill

But when it comes
Then all that we hold dear
Can be put in a thimble
Rolled flat in the rear

When the end comes
Our life we will borrow
For after that time
There will be no tomorrow

THE END OF TIME WE WILL
NEVER SEE

The end of time
We will never see
When it doth come
We will not be

The end of all we know
Will pass before our eyes
We may wish to keep it all
But it will us despise

When the end comes
All that we hold dear
Will not matter to ourselves
Eternity will be here

THE END OF TIME IS COMING

The end of time is coming
But it is not here
When all shall pass away
The forces of darkness will cheer

The days of our time are numbered
Their power shall pass away
For the power of the good
Shall hold eternal sway

The good shall be happy
If by the light of good they live
For the power of good continues
Has eternal life to give

ON WINNING AND LOSING

There is winning and losing
And how you play the game
There are accolades for the winner
But over time, it's all the same

When you win it feels so good
That you could walk on air
When you lose you feel so bad
That you could cease to care

But winning and losing are not final
They don't define the game
In the future you will remember
They both will be the same

The object should be winning
Losing is a shame
But you will find what is important
That you played the game

WINNING IS EVERYTHING

"Winning is everything"
So the coach says
But winning within the rules
Is what he means

The cost of winning
Can be quite high
But in later years
You may ask "Why"

For winning and sacrificing our self
By pain and by cutting the soul
Will make the body go dim
But we must be made whole

ON WINNING AND LOSING FOR US

There's winning and losing for us
And how we play the game
Some say it doesn't matter
We all wind up just the same

Winning is better than losing
On that we all can agree
The end of the game
Is for all humankind to see

But winning by nefarious means
Will in the mind of men
Blacken our memory
Until time does end

THE IMPERATIVE THEREFORE

There are many things
That the speaker would have us do
They give many arguments
Some false, some true

They tell us what we should do
Of reasons for us to act
They present many arguments
Some a little short on fact

The speaker says that "A" is true
And so it is with "B"
Therefore, because of these
We shoul
d do "C"

We may all agree with "A"
And believe that "B" is true
But the actions - the imperative therefore
Are actions we should never never do

So before you begin to march
And head off a cliff
Consider the results of your actions
Do not be deaf

TIME

We act and we wait
For the future to come
When we act time goes fast
When we wait, it doesn't run

We have only so much time
To do what we must do
To the goal we act
To the end that's true

Time is in the action
Of us and of machine
That clicks off the seconds
The period in between

EAST AND WEST

East is east and west is west
And never the twain shall meet
But what they all agree on
Everyone has to eat

The things that divide us
Are rooted in the past
The things that make us one
Are our everlasting task

The task that makes us one
Is the human need
It is mercy and justice
For which we plead

Governments which are not just
Systems that crush the frail
Are systems and governments
That will, that must fail

WHERE ARE YOU GOING?

Where are you going?
A question to ask
If you know the answer
You can set your task

If you know your destination
If you know your direction
You can aim for that future
Without deflection

This is often not the case
We judge progress
By the speed not the direction
And may, in the process, regress

So know where you are going
In life and each day
Your life will be lived
You will succeed as you may

WHERE HAVE YOU BEEN?

Where are you going?
Where have you been?
Offer an explanation
Know where to begin

Love your neighbor
As you love yourself
Do good to all
With love and help

Know where you are going
Know where you have been
Do good to all
God save us from sin

THERE IS MANY A WORD

There is many a word
That we have heard
That leads us to distraction
And many a thought
That we have bought
That leads us into action

There is one word
Have you heard?
That word is work
And we can find
To do what we mind
If we do not shirk

This is the point retort
Of this poem short
That we find meaning in the doing
If all thoughts be true
It is what we do
Doing is better than talking

THEY SAY

They say they want the truth
That is what they say
If the truth flatters them
They will be willing to pay

So search for the truth
To know the good end
For as we go through life
We can know how to begin

But if the truth is not flattering
If it exposes their warts
You'd best be prepared for the worst
Because, as they say, "the truth hurts"

NO EMPIRE LASTS FOREVER

No empire lasts forever
No matter how strong
They will pay the price
For what they did wrong

Injustice comes around
For those who did it so
They were once powerful
So the oppressed know

The past makes the present
The present makes the future
With surgical success
All history to structure

So do the justice you know
The future will you hold
When the future becomes the present
The past will haunt you when you're old

THE NEW

Criticism is to be expected
Whenever there's something new
The basic concern of others
"This is not what we do"

No matter the concept
No matter how good
The old way worked
The new way just could

So changes come slowly
To humankind and to the world
But it is the bottom line
Which does progress's flag unfurl

INTEGRITY

Integrity is a ten dollar word
A word we all desire
In those with whom we deal
No matter if the results are dire

Everyone has integrity
Upon which their reputation depend
If we compromise our self
Then scorn upon us will descend

Some buy and sell others
Making them do your will
By money, drugs or threats
Sometimes a bitter pill

Once you've sold your integrity
Once you've sold your very self
You cannot buy your freedom
You cannot cleanse yourself

TIME TRAVEL

Time is a concept
That connects events together
It talks about causality
What happens ever

Without events
Without causality
There would be no time
No reality

So when we talk
Of traveling in time
We talk of moving
The pattern, the rhyme

To go to the past
Is to insert
Energy in that place
That would hurt

To go to the future
Is no great feat
We do it all the time
New events we meet

So if we could travel in time
To the past and reset the clock
Some present event
We could easily block

But that minor disruption
Might cause a discontinuity
The world as we know it
Would lose continuity

So if we ever can
Go into the past
We might find our world
Would never last

CONFLICT

There is disagreement
There is discord
All this is conflict
A distorted chord

Sometimes conflict is bad
Sometimes it is good
It depends on how it's used
Depends on what we would

So sow the seeds of conflict
There's a wide range
For within every conflict
There are the seeds of change

HATE

Hate is an evil bug
It eats at our very soul
Causing us to lose sleep
Destroying what makes us whole

We can hate anyone
Hate with a passion
Try to give it vent
Whenever it is in fashion

When hate is given vent
When we let it take to action
We condemn ourselves
To final destruction

ABOUT THE AUTHOR

Richard Gold was born in Bartow, Florida and attended college at the University of South Florida. He retired from the Government and has been writing poems for a long time. His late mother, Rachel Gold, was also a poet and wrote numerous poems about many things. Gold presently lives in Indian Head, Maryland with his wife Penelope Gold, an accomplished artist.

www.ingramcontent.com/pod-product-compliance
Lightning Source LLC
Chambersburg PA
CBHW032216040426
42449CB00005B/626